ACCIDENTALS IN THE MAIN

ACCIDENTALS IN THE MAIN

CLARE BRANT

Shoestring Press

Printed by imprintdigital
Upton Pyne, Exeter
www.imprintdigital.com

Typesetting and cover design by narrator
www.narrator.me.uk
info@narrator.me.uk
033 022 300 39

Published by Shoestring Press
19 Devonshire Avenue, Beeston, Nottingham, NG9 1BS
(0115) 925 1827
www.shoestringpress.co.uk

First published 2016

Cover image: Neptune's Jewel Box by Gooding, 1989

ISBN 978-1-905208-67-0

Dear Helena —
Sharing much love
now & ahead
with Roz love too
xxxx

Clare

for

Gooding
(1960-2016)

– artist, observer, practical expert, true friend.

2 December 2016

CONTENTS

Absolutist	1
Antiquary at a Window	2
Artist in Residence	3
Belief in Crocodiles	4
Bird Box	5
Brevity	6
Coconut and Crab	7
Coming Home	8
Cui Bono	9
Dance	10
Dawn	11
Deerhound Return	12
Encounter	13
Enough	14
Et in Arcadia Ego	15
Four Horsemen and Me	16
From His Coy Mistress	17
Ghost of Christmas Past	18
Golden Age	19
Heatwave	20
Hug-me-tight	21
Jam Tomorrow	22
Jubilee	23
Kunduz Runner	24
Last Days	25
Lighter	26
Meteor Could Wipe Out Earth, Says Expert	27
Missing Word	28
Nocturne	29
Palinode	30
Pax Deorum, the Peace of the Gods	31
Pulse	32
Pride	33
Question, Pending	34
Raindrop	35
Rameau at the Coliseum	36

Ripeness 37
Rowan 38
Searching 39
Slow Waltz Out of the Room 40
Solitude 41
Sometimes 42
St. Pancras Crypt 43
St. Peter Healing the Sick with his Shadow, c.1427 44
Tennyson's Brook 45
The Illuminator of Drains 46
The Miller's Tale 47
The News in Wiltshire 48
They Were Expensive, These Lilies 49
Threat 50
Twilight 51
Vanishing Point 52
Vespers 53
Victoria Plum 54
Vintage Velvets 55
When Winter Nights Draw in 56
You Don't Know the Half of It 57

ABSOLUTIST

Talons, beaks and great hooked claws
scoop and grip bewildered being

this is punishment
harsh

what's betrayed by narrowed eyes
power and fear

plump satin cushion
bed of nails

in the next life the beggar at the gate
turns up again

cruelty's ready
scimitar sharp.

ANTIQUARY AT A WINDOW

Antiquary begins in *enceinte* wall (thirteenth century)
whose white doves flutter in and out of loopholes

reliquary begins with primroses nestled on the bank below
almost all one in profusion

on the landing a brown pottery jug
(nineteenth century) holds primrose flowers

originally the village lay round the church
now parkland covers houses, taverns, shops

where the turf swells ewes
ovine opine, ruminant, chew contented

it comes together as things fall apart
antiquary, reliquary, understanding clasped.

ARTIST IN RESIDENCE

The spider who lives between window frame
and drainpipe
trembles in the rain

sees comings and goings
visitors, postman
moods

under attenuated skies
she plies her patient net
attentive

her well-fed body is supported
by herself and atmosphere
tutelar deity, raconteur.

BELIEF IN CROCODILES

In the background is an island
where boys gang up with torments
it was mine before they arrived
with their nets of myth and sharp sticks
I had the odd fish to snap at
sands to myself
patrolling was nonchalant
I whistled and sang to the bees

now indigestibility
sits in my craw
life by the clock
tick tock
tick tock
they all know where I am
old block, tick tock

my sidlings are spoiled
temper turned in
I am stuck in tick tock
slave to clock
it sits in my gut, shock
brinnnnnng
alarm of clock

no more in praise of scaly, gnarly, snarly
I am ticked off
by mock of clock
tick-tock o'clock
hiccup will not dislodge it
while they, stupid children,
gather round a gnat and clap for joy

I am a creature with no vision of transcendence
philosophy has metal hands, clock clutch
rasping cogs
clap your hands if you believe in crocodiles.

BIRD BOX

Under the eaves the sparrows come and go
twittering street news

a feeder in this garden's full
a shadow of red kite passed by

thrush chicks have fledged
the squirrel's resting in her ash tree dray

the sparrows push and chatter
and yes, they noticed

a birch bird box appeared
inviting

please come and make a home
that human crisis, so lamentable, preventable, of housing

does not apply to this permissive plot
come take up residence and thrive.

BREVITY

Days of wine and roses
must plenitude slide?

wine and roses yet to come
cellared bottle, rose in bud

days of wine and roses gone
fallen petals, empty glass.

COCONUT AND CRAB

Once I came up from a dive
and found I'd surfaced eye to eye
with a small coconut

bobbing, in leaf
cradling in its shoot
a tiny, shiny crab

all hail adventurer!
Both crab and I were startled
it shot away to dark side of its moon

I tried to reassure it
castaway navigator
I did not mean to interrupt your epic journey

we are such accidentals in the main
coconut conquistadors
heading for fresh land.

COMING HOME

When the traveller returns it is strange
to see pots of geraniums close to the door that is home
looking as if change had not changed them.

Key in the lock opens a door into familiarity
which has changed in ways that change nothing.

A suitcase carried in says firmly
change happened
look here are souvenirs and presents
clothes to be washed
books that were taken and read.

Here is the telephone, through which
safe return must be told as news and rejoicings.

All of this revolves so powerfully
the traveller must sit down to grasp
this moment, in which change turns
to continuity
and continuity returns.

CUI BONO

A nurse who attends to the dying
passes conclusions on
what we say at the end
summation

I wish I'd had the courage to live true to me
I wish I hadn't worked so hard
I wish I'd had the courage to express my feelings
I wish I'd stayed in touch with friends

our consummations, summarised
I wish I'd let myself be happier

after I'd read this I walked out
into a pink streak sunset
twilight cool by the canal

there are many houses full of books
lamps turn on and greenish streetlight
illuminates the evening

I wish myself happier
letting be
letting wish be happier
true, happy me.

DANCE

~ Dominique Mercy, principal in Tanztheater Wuppertal

His eyes glance sideways
his mouth is down
uncertain

his glance straightens
his hands flex
his shoulders pull up slightly lightly

a thought has crossed his mind
a thought has crossed my mind
we know a feeling and it straightens

our glance is look, direct
what next
next flexes, gladly uncertain.

DAWN

At dawn one blackbird shouts a signal
suddenly the hedges, roofs and air
are filled with chorus

we slept while it threw circles in the lake of light
trills and echoes widened out allusively
the day flowed smoothly as a bolt of silk.

DEERHOUND RETURN

In nuances of grey and silver
the durable and mortal coexist

that courtesy which deerhounds took up long ago
comes coursing, swift across the kingcup meadow.

ENCOUNTER

Unexpectedly a fox on the path
stock-still in streetlight

shimmer of joy
I stopped in my tracks

shiver of wild
bushy tail vanished

I went on, stirred

a few yards on light slid and hid
under the black-lapped bridge

a sooty wall barged up
path righted itself

glimpse of an animal gaze
eye glint in bushes, starred.

ENOUGH

I am old enough to cry when death
snatches away someone I love

I am old enough to be half-shamed by tears in public
I bite my lip

I tilt my head to look at sky as if it had some answer
to be battened on by blinking

a room slips pooling
clouds grow diamond-fringed

I couldn't tell you why
this urge to hide

why grief must stay inside
you're old enough to know

except a fear that if it all came out
I would be old enough no more

I would be infant, hopelessly bewildered
I would be ancient, fated haplessly to die

old enough to know the ripping by a storm
takes trees of any age

old enough to know
that old is never long enough

that tears will stream
to sculpt a landscape not in view

grief carries underground
an echo, not enough of you.

ET IN ARCADIA EGO

The lover returned with his beloved
to the rocks and chasm where he carved her name
again and again
her name

the scars of his heart still fresh
devotion palpable

beloved, he cried, does not your heart
beat faster, beat stronger
to be in a place so full of you?

Let us go, she said, mon ami
the air here is not good for me

neither novel nor rock records
why she turned away
shades of obelisk and cypress
slant across a sepulchre

again and again her name
Arcadia
Et in Ego.

FOUR HORSEMEN AND ME

One day someone may say why didn't you write about
the poor, the war, the horrific
tragic specifics of these days?

The rich in glossy limousines
slide from canapés to kobu beef
while orphans liquidize in their own bodies

lesions, wounds, the soulless stare of trauma
mines, decapitations, bombs in markets
thumps and bangs and shakes of power-hungry madness
splintered bones and stumps and red raw flesh

The bloody men are mounting up
it is true
I confess
I prefer unicorns.

FROM HIS COY MISTRESS

Forms that change forgot to change
cycad woodlouse shark
show there might have been
a world so perfectly designed
you could subtract from time
the change that says time is

creatures under polar ice
grow imperceptibly, so slow
so leisurely your mind falls off in chunks
while they grow slowly on
to vastness in the dark
so slow a millimetre takes a decade

I could compare all this to love
I could contrast the ingenuity
with which my species tears away
inventing as it swarms
lantern, amputation saw, grenades
nearly perfect hand-held generation

cycad woodlouse shark
what do we know of love?

GHOST OF CHRISTMAS PAST

Where along the way did Christmas with its sparkly tree
its icicles and silver stars
where did it acquire the ghost of Christmas past?

Firelight flickers into other hearths
I have a tangerine unpeeling feeling
lost ones are with me again

I almost lay another place at table
knowing you have left the feast.

GOLDEN AGE

Some thought we were golden and maybe we were
who can tell, now
when the survivors still cough in the night
salt water, welled from the deep

all the tides since, spring and neep
cannot alter that tarred line of foreshore
where crabs scuttle fiercely and sticky anemones
plant sturdiness in accidents of rockpool

let it all go, all the pain
recriminations, praise, blame, love
all the reasons that our hearts beat faster
all the tears, the justifications

it no longer matters
tell the rushes
let seagull cry
carry away our chorus of grief

where the snow falls royally
where the dandelion roots, loyally
there is the soil
where we meet.

HEATWAVE

It's been described before, this roar of sun that scorches through
the grass and burns the leaves
this sear of heat is nothing new

nor indolence too lazy to find words
even as it stirs to think of getting a cold drink

the dog finds cool in temporary ways
flat out on tiles in mimicry of one-too-many from the night before
his heavy sleep is furred

in bulky, sweaty reveries comes new respect for sun
it translates reasons to get nothing done.

HUG-ME-TIGHT

Every day there are mutations in your cells
runes rewriting genes
arrhythmic algorhythmia

on castle walls a tiny fern
says hug-me-tight to stone
precarious and perilous

one day you'll get an exit number
terminus completion date
and every day till then sneers best by

green leaf carnival
red leaf festival
brown leaf poised to fall

I came, I saw, I wrote
I grew, I flowered, I faded
root matrix in white channel of blank stone.

JAM TOMORROW

Some forms of spoiling are commutable
mould on the surface of jam, for instance
is unimportant

I skim a nasty email with a sense
that time would be much better spent
making jam that did not spoil

strawberries, sifted sugar, a big fine pot
veteran wooden spoon
generosity of purpose

halfway through the vision I remember
jam can scald
as malice does

there's still this email
prolonged exposure to moulds for
instance in a workplace is harmful

some moulds are cultured
they, I find
are least commutable.

JUBILEE

A chilly wind whips through the bunting
bringing rain over us

competitive cakes are mouldering already
bearskin soldiers' march suspended

it is grey and cold and wet
no dampener on sycophancy

the richest woman in the world rides by
be grateful for a nod and wave

o majesty how gracious in a sea of pageant
history empire bleating from the telly

we commoners should revel in ourselves
the rain it raineth on just cause

radicals sing stirring protests
huddled at the Crown & Anchor.

KUNDUZ RUNNER

Red rose that scents the air of summer nights
drifts upward from this woven thread

I have unrolled a carpet
a rug to run the length of hall

come in, it says, we join in flowering
let me show you how life lays out rhythm and a flow

weaving in the future footfall
press of thorns and crush of rose

I will spread your possibilities in moments
I am the geometry of where you want to go.

LAST DAYS

Old age is courage, fear, husking of aims
dandelion clock, slowly undock
countdown to blowaway
shiver of gone

there is so much sleeping
open-mouthed astonishment
marvellous procession
steely dispossession.

LIGHTER

The lighter that I pick up from the pavement
has lit up someone else's habits, tedium and ease
smudgily it carries fingerprints
cautiously I finger it
no obvious owner in the passers by
and so I pocket it
finders keepers

Tonight it lies upon my kitchen table
I want it to begin a conversation
I want to purge it of associations
rush-hour crowds and dull delays of trains
a thousand lives convergent
bedbugs feeding on a city mattress

it's quarter-used
and I'm half-witted with imagining its purchaser

flick click it flashes on me
the weightiness of lighter.

METEOR COULD WIPE OUT EARTH, SAYS EXPERT

Suppose there was a meteor
careening in a whirl through outer space
it nears the earth and in an accidental quirk
of gravity shaves a sliver off the angle
in which it hurtles closer
through blue-black sky to azure plain and ocean blue below

give it a chance encounter with another rock in similar free fall
it twists and has a new course
it plummets to a city
that happens to be yours
your town your street your house your home
it's heading for your roof
inexorable

what slow and dreamy words will come upon you
to shape the knowledge that you're done?

MISSING WORD

Knowledge we know is no protection
no prophylactic, no consolation
no tactic's diversion or action's aversion
budges this stone

no paper or string wraps up this thing
it has sharp edges
it will not stop singing
it hurts the air

if we join hand-in-hand in a ring
nursery rhyme spin
it walks to the back of the room
from where it looks on, arms folded

if we draw the curtains and lock doors
it cleans the bath and changes sheets
humouring your need
with a tune hummed to itself

whether you go out or stay in
it has a coat to hand or matching slippers
the only thing it will not copy
is the missing word.

NOCTURNE

Spendthrift of windfall you
pop the possibilities
in champagne cork flights
that never land

these firework stars say nothing of burnt fingers
they momentarily hang
above the burned bridge lands
and fall invisibly in cinders.

PALINODE

Things I have left undone
long list of loss
arguments I never won
a stone that gathered green moss

I went rolling along the beach
I was washed to and fro by the tides
glass-sealed dream in a bottle
braving ocean to be by your side.

PAX DEORUM, THE PEACE OF THE GODS

The ancients didn't have pockets
on account of which
no pocket books
no pickpockets

no pocketing of bribes
perhaps they put things up their toga sleeves
I see you slip that secret elbow-wards
a crook of arm to harbour furtive gains

in my pockets I have keys and coins
I still need ancient virtues
dignity, integrity, humanity
a wish for justice

with hands in pockets I stand and look about me
for pax deorum, all that I would be.

PULSE

Flightpath zoom and rustle were the signs
deep in a tangle of clematis
green shoots mauve flowers
a nest

it looked empty
then six hatchlings rose up, yellow-throated
squeaking agape
feed me feed me feed me

at night they have been privy
to the court of a rueful queen
who rules over nodding poppies
and foxgloves chimed by rhymes of rain

peony sceptre, rose coronet
white fireworks of scent rise all around
the youngsters stare, crowding
for a glimpse of growing moon

questioned about the future I equivocate
it's mayfly season, sparrow time
arrivals and departures mingle
pulse of summer coming on.

PRIDE

The child who is dancing round the garden pond
has seen a toad
angel, angel, she's yelling
angelically

and the toad who has heard itself called by name
hops happily away.

QUESTION, PENDING

Will I ever hear from you again?
The question hangs
a coathanger shifting in closet

I long for it to disappear
I hold a wish contrarily close
a dangle jangle yes, please yes

coathanger twist and triangle
the question slants another angle
will you ever hear again from me?

RAINDROP

Raindrops hang pendant on long blades of grass
rain has passed on
a group of geese feed across the middle distance
necks arched, alert

through the gate is a field
where rabbits populate the evening paths
blackberries glisten
sweetened by the rain

you are elsewhere but I hold you close
translucent as amber
slow tears of syrup on a cherry tree

in the slowness of drops
unwilling to go
I see attachments shelter
gravity acknowledged

our world is raindrop
crystal globe
tiny, enormous in close up
full, transient, unwilling to go.

RAMEAU AT THE COLISEUM

~ Castor et Pollux

Mock-Roman madness rears in masks
bronze horses plunge toward the pit
cream, gold and crimson fall in swags

it's hard to grasp the plot, all gods and heroes
running round in upsets
and forever farewells which last five minutes

why so much made of brothers
so little of sisters
cherchez la femme, mes hommes, mes dieux

we peer through telescopes
at our favourites
willing them on to decide aright

which they do not
which is what we have come to see
we are comforted

as singing soars we too cast cliché to the winds
appassionata, we surrender to the night's black cloak
red satin death rises in magnificence

our stage is set for cheering and applause
Roman horses plunge by crimson swags
we are enlightened by the exits of farewell.

RIPENESS

Ripen in fruit bowl
says the label on a plastic punnet
of apricots still psychically attached to tree

in coming days they'll let attachments go, blushing
they'll soften, by some alchemy of air
that plumps them full of juiciness

china clay was spun so they could rest and nest
revolving shades of peach and orange
that settle and resolve in apricot

a dimple hints they're cute
belying bite

we cultivate the flush of youth
then we mature, ripening in fruit bowl.

ROWAN

With the archbishop's poems in her pocket
she walked over needles and knelt on rocks

crown of thorny roses touched her head
blessings pressed in

thicket and wood, aspirations in the night
justice and mercy, light divined

let me share with you what I am
it is a consolation, perfect trust.

SEARCHING

I have forgotten what I came here for
this roomy place is full of things that give no clue

was it for this

I have forgotten what I came here for
was it for this, forbearance?

SLOW WALTZ OUT OF THE ROOM

They have all gone now, those old family friends
who breezed in for a gin and chinwag
arriving with gifts and due warning

they did useful things in the war
one in polkadot and floppy hat drove ambulances
one had been a spy

the war rolled out there like fog
punctured by aircraft thrusting up from the sea
oily and gasping

they referred to it glancingly, behind them
we wondered why.

SOLITUDE

When I am melancholy I want solitude
run in cool water over a bruise
it soothes

when thrashing subsides and threshing takes over
I wonder why the sunset hurt so much

all the names, all the stones
ghosting the air
with griefs no longer precise

so water softens stone
obduracy rounds, river smooth

through waterfall of hidden frictions
fictions of the self in solitude.

SOMETIMES

Sometimes I wonder if my cracked heart
can bear
any more
hammer blows
of loss

Sometimes I feel the tulips bearing up
the arch of larch cones
unpeeling in their purple and fresh green
a fluted spring

Sometimes the acts of balance wobble
unsteady hands
clasp lovingly
the hands
I must let go

Sometimes I call the lost ones close
to murmur
of the woes
they did not live
to see

Sometimes I scatter blossom in a wilful passing
so petals fall
and spell
white lettered growth
of soul.

ST. PANCRAS CRYPT

~ 'Lost but not forgotten': an installation by Jane Wildgoose

Cold air rose from the floor
shades and shadows
crept toward eternity

where ink and feathers plumed black mouldy walls
signs cryptic in stone
spoke of that loss we call I miss you

white flowers defied droop, branching out
to warmer air and laughter
gleam of a wine glass, breath of life

in careful hands death lives again
the living are grateful for hair's breadth deliverance
the dead rise up in their hair's breadth attachments.

ST. PETER HEALING THE SICK WITH HIS SHADOW, c.1427

~ after Masaccio

There's a boy with withered legs
his chin jutted in suffering
next to him a man with a crutch
and a man, half-naked, sick

behind them masonry, arches, windows
walls bobbled by sunlight
slant in stone towers

it is broad daylight
not that anyone cares
whitewashed walls stare blankly at the sun

a holy man walks down the street
gaze like a blind man
his shadow falls
not where you expect it.

TENNYSON'S BROOK

Tennyson I thank you for writing your song of a river
beginning with bickering brook
I come from haunts of coot and fern

we read it aloud in class, aged eight
five stanzas each
and ever after

I come from haunts of coot and hern
I make a sudden sally
And sparkle out among the fern
To bicker down a valley

I come from haunts of coot and fern
I make a sudden sally
To something something something
and bicker down the valley

sometimes I like my version best
something, something, something
flows water-like, downhill.

THE ILLUMINATOR OF DRAINS

Into this frame of day what might we cram
among the wallflowers and the speedwell
your famous kin evaporate to footnotes
winding to that future which upturns the present
as daisies do dead bodies

underneath our feet the drains run crookedly and true
in darkness whose drip-drip splashes melodies for rats

we go there sometimes, consciously
and sometimes it finds us, disturbing even ground
as tree roots push out under headstones
while life goes on, in leaps and bounds
in coil, uncoil of underground

the marvel is that death and life walk hand in hand
to sit in parks canoodling

and in the cheerful air of birdsong
you wouldn't know the trees in blossom
touch with their deepest filaments the cracks
where scum cries longingly for light
and spores yearn lightly for a breeze to carry upward

through nets of soil, decay which day dispels
like ancestry and pride, perennials' perfume.

THE MILLER'S TALE

for Jonty Carter

Miller says the wheels have special sounds
that ravel as they turn around and round
so that he knows if aught's amiss
and when and where to fix the creak or hiss

Miller says the power of flour
exceeds capacity of dynamite
to blow the stone from towers
and powder rubble with unearthly white

Miller says that flour's motes
a terpsichore of dancing notes
a backlit fall of flourish spores
take four full hours to settle to the floor

Miller says he must work in the dark
by shadow fall on whitewash wall
lest spark ignite a fatal brawl
of wood and wood, and kill

him too who gives his life to this old mill
he, the last who understands
the grind of millstone, flour ingrained in hands
the rush of water and its turn of wheel
lumbering and smoothing, soothing
dialect of oak in dialogue with stream
the force of guidance guided
history powering dream.

THE NEWS IN WILTSHIRE

Downland rolls out its ode to joy
severed head sings on the radio
the children have no bread
pub signs swing by, cider festival
drink deep, all welcome
the children have no milk
who has the high ground?

Lilting hills hold songs of war
barbaric spreads among us
the children have no water
downland holds severed head, no water
joy dries in us
joy dries in the children
and in the severed head.

THEY WERE EXPENSIVE, THESE LILIES

When the flowers came out they said
here's recompense
in purest white gigantic blooms

they gestured loosely to some other fate
backstage in diva's dressing room
grand foyer, richly perfuming hotel

to make the most of where they are
they let their petals open
like doves who fan advantage of the sun

dimpled, curled and crinkled, plate-size flowers
six-anthered strong and proud
with pod-assured succession of success

they give extravagant rebuke to their observer
worth is self-evident: be confident.

THREAT

~ To an old tune

Is the corpse in the corner detective or thug?
Are there signs of a struggle – cracked glass, broken jug?
Take care
Take care
There's a man in the shadows who waits on the stairs

Can you count on your friends when the going gets tough?
Do you know of a safe house or must you sleep rough?
Take care
Take care
There's a man in the shadows who creeps up the stairs

When the tread creaks outside where will you hide
Will you cower in a cold sweat afraid and wide-eyed?
Take care
Take care
The man knows your secret and it's too late for prayers.

TWILIGHT

There is still light in the sky at an hour
impossibly late for light in the sky

first star appears pointedly
above the rose leaf silhouettes

the octogenarians look out of their windows
for light in the sky

on an evening when afterglow
brightens the heavy of impossible

there are surprises, stars
imprinted, light against sky

we are full of possible
lightly improvised.

VANISHING POINT

~ Seasalter

The sea brings something like an open hand
that stretches out to take away your troubles
along the bright beach light strolls up
to lighten cares and make you carefree
the world you know is gone and in its place
refresh flows in with little waves within
so frets forget to say their names

in prints of sand and weathering, in sea-gnawed groynes, in
ruined shells
time crunches anciently
in tides that press the coast with curves
in easy breeze that helps the waves turn back again
to where they came from
it is a place we know
from where we came, to where we go.

VESPERS

By the bed in the morning was catsuit
dogsuit
tigerskin
asses' ears

she wove red feathers in her long dark hair
remora waved goodbye to her

when the moon peeped through dark branches
she was inordinate

waterborne, with silver pools and indigo depths
pearlescent

glitter of sunshine on the bedroom window
duckdown and fur
suitable for morning
catsuit, dogsuit.

VICTORIA PLUM

Fanning new branches from a tall strong graft she waits looped
for a coronation
I know she's the one
so I carry her tenderly in my arms
to a car she can hardly fit into

we drive home gently
rough bumps do shake the darling buds
sorry Your Highness
nothing grand awaits you
except a garden full of love

the future floats across in sprays of blossom
longevity, painterly, homage to art
delicate screen print of cognates
plumb centre, plumly aplomb
empire of birds

harvests in armfuls, purpled and plump
sweetness of juice oozing sticky and shared with wasps
impromptu, immediate dessert
bubbling crumble, ruby jam
summer preserved

what fruit I will give away, rejoicing
in lusciousness on neighbours' doorsteps
what roots she will send to the earth I'll inherit
her leaves and shoots will come and go for years
and when I'm gone, she'll flourish on.

VINTAGE VELVETS

Do you think the suddenly dark sky
has any idea we have changed the clocks
black inklings, maybe

escarpment backbone, bumpy
beech leaves are leaving the trees so carelessly
it could be a lesson

there is softness in your voice of cashmere, tweed
browns and neutrals, oatmeal, wool
purpose in your step across the grass

some frontier moves forward
blue turns to midnight blue to black
vintage velvets of the mind.

WHEN WINTER NIGHTS DRAW IN

What are those things that I shall do
when winter nights draw in

the tidied shelves, the polished stove
cleared-out cupboards, mended clothes
when winter nights draw in

but then the dark and cold will press
resolve will freeze
and efforts falter to a halt, default

it's then that indolence attends
to sampling of sloe gin.

YOU DON'T KNOW THE HALF OF IT

Too clever by half
that won't do, oh no
slosh a bit out, level up –
still over that line?

Too clever by quarter
which is three quarters short
of twice as clever –
level up, slosh a bit out?

Lines hover round pretty stupid
a mark, one up from a thumbprint
a smudge to encourage
a fluid ounce average?

Will it do and for who
why should you draw in like snail horns
your full range of abilities
luck of the draw?

Too clever by half
clever times two
split the difference
so long as we get somewhere true?